VINTAGE
GEORGIA
SIGNS

Welcome, welcome, one and all! Say, how do you feel about corrugated yellow plastic as a background for signage? You'd better love it, because this is far from the only example of it you are about to see.

VINTAGE

GEORGIA SIGNS

TIM HOLLIS

THE
History
PRESS

Published by The History Press
Charleston, SC
www.historypress.com

First published 2024

Manufactured in the United States

ISBN 9781467155793

Library of Congress Control Number: 2024931852

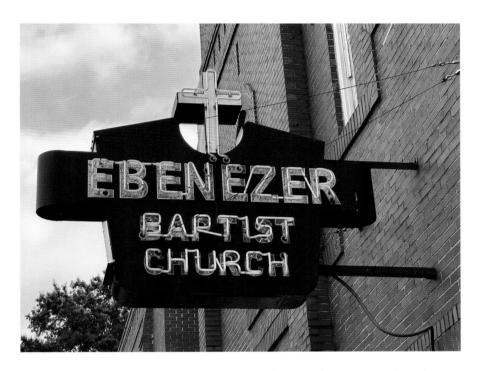

Atlanta's Ebenezer Baptist Church is most famous for being the pastorate of Martin Luther King Jr. during the 1960s (and his father for decades before that). This neon sign was first added to the church around the time of the transition from father to son and was restored to its original glory about twenty years ago. *Stephanie Stuckey collection.*

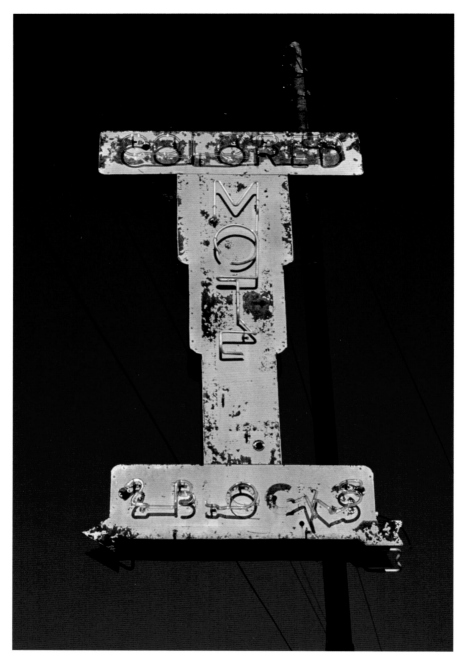

One of the many problems Dr. King was trying to correct can be illustrated by this crumbling sign found by photographer John Margolies in Statesboro. By the early 1980s, the broken neon was difficult to read, but apparently this "colored motel" was a couple of blocks off the main drag. *John Margolies collection.*

CONTENTS

What did we tell you about corrugated yellow plastic? This example—and it won't be the last—stood above the "gull wing" canopy of the Stuckey's just south of Macon on I-75. *Gord Booth collection.*

FOREWORD

Step back in time and explore the captivating world of vintage signs—where history meets architectural artistry. The signs showcased in this book transcend mere works of art; they stand as silent witnesses to the past, each bearing a unique story of a bygone era.

Traveling the backroads of Georgia with Tim Hollis is akin to an expedition with a modern-day Indiana Jones, scouring small towns and cities for hidden treasures. Yet our quest is not for the Ark of the Covenant but rather a single-arch McDonald's sign. In our world of sign hunting, stumbling upon the neon glow of a Wishbone Fried Chicken feels like striking gold.

The images that grace these pages freeze in time a fading America. An original Taco Bell sign, an inconspicuous relic, sits unassumingly amidst the hustle of Savannah's Victory Drive, sandwiched between a Wendy's and an Arby's. Like the iconic Big Chicken in Marietta and the scarce remaining Krispy Kreme crowns, these signs are survivors, defiant against the tide of urban development, shouting, "Look at me!" as hurried motorists pass by.

But Tim Hollis doesn't pass by; he slams on his brakes and pulls over—every time. Thanks to him, alongside notables like famed photographer John Margolies, meticulous archivist Debra Jane Seltzer of RoadArch.com, Rolando Pujol's Retroligist Instagram posts and the Society for Commercial Archeology's photo library, these remarkable signs are chronicled and celebrated. Much credit is owed to these rare individuals who "get it" when it comes to signs. They understand that ours is a calling to save a vanishing part of America.

We are the sign enthusiasts, the ones who cannot contain our excitement at the sight of a rare Rexall Drugs sign, a perfectly preserved midcentury modern theater marquee or a rare Norge ball dry cleaning sign. Navigating the signs featured in this remarkable book is akin to a treasure hunt across our state. I invite you to not only peruse these pages from the comfort of your home but also to hit the road and explore with this book as your traveling companion. A road trip is about savoring the journey. Pull over and enjoy these special signs in their natural habitat, capture your own photos and share them. Become a part of our sign community; together, we can save our signs and also save a piece of what's special about our state.

Stephanie Stuckey
Chair
Stuckey's Corporation

ACKNOWLEDGEMENTS

Although much of the material you will see in the pages that follow originated in my own decades-long collection of memorabilia, kudos must be given to the additional sources that enlivened the result. As you will notice in the credit lines for the photos, a number of them (as well as other helpful information) came from fellow tourism collectors, historians and photographers: Gord Booth; Nelson Boyd; Tim Campbell; Al Coleman; Andy Duckett; Debra Jane Seltzer (www.roadarch.com); Ron Sherman; David M. Smith; Stephanie Stuckey; Michael Sussman; the Vintage Atlanta Facebook group; and Russell Wells.

We must also acknowledge the late photographer John Margolies, who bequeathed his personal archive to the Library of Congress with the amazing stipulation that no restrictions were to be imposed on its use by other authors and researchers.

These two photos illustrate part of this book's origin. The top image was taken by yours truly in 1968, at age five, with his pappy posing by the Palms Court sign in Waycross. I did not return to Waycross until 1992, at which time I found the sign still standing and virtually unchanged (although with the addition of a Sonny's BBQ across the street). All traces of the Palms Court and its sign have now been obliterated (and Papa Hollis passed away in 1995).

INTRODUCTION

S ome of you might be familiar with another of my books, *Lost Attractions of Georgia* (2021). If so, please look at this one not so much as a sequel but a companion volume. While the two do tread somewhat similar paths, you will find that this one branches out into territory *Lost Attractions* never explored.

Before we get into the first chapter, perhaps it is wise to give a little explanation as to what this book does not contain. The vast majority of the vintage Georgia signs discussed in the pages that follow no longer exist—or, if they do, there had to be a good reason to include them anyway. Some of you might wonder why such Georgia landmarks as the KFC Big Chicken in Marietta or the famed "Fly Delta Jets" neon sign at the Atlanta airport were left out. The main reason is a simple one: we can all still see them in person. (Now, if a photo could have been located showing the Big Chicken when it was the emblem of the Johnny Reb's Restaurant, in the building's pre-KFC days, it would certainly have taken its proper place.)

And that brings up another reason your favorite sign, past or present, might not be here—namely, no photo of it could be found, or if it could, there was no way to ascertain its publication rights. A third, but more minor, reason is that quite a few signs were a part of the aforementioned *Lost Attractions of Georgia*, and in the interest of variety, we have attempted as little duplication as possible. When it was necessary to illustrate a sign that had already appeared in the earlier book, we at least tried to choose a different angle of it.

Since you were intelligent enough to pick up this book in the first place, you most likely could figure out its format just by reading the table of contents. Just as any road trip needs a map, though (whether the Rand McNally type or a smartphone's screen), here we will take a few minutes to plot out where we will be going.

Chapter 1 concerns itself with signage related to shopping, whether huge department stores or their more modest five-and-ten cousins. In chapter 2, we move into nearly everyone's favorite topic, food, covering restaurant signage as well as advertisements for various grocery products. (Not surprisingly, Coca-Cola looms large in Georgia.) Chapter 3 moves on to the topic of automotive-related signs, including gas stations and others of their ilk. Naturally enough, in chapter 4 we stop for the night at examples of the many types of motels along the Georgia roadside, from independent mom-and-pop operations to giants such as Holiday Inn.

The final two chapters are the ones with the most foggily defined boundaries; chapter 5 deals with Georgia tourism (trying to avoid stepping on *Lost Attractions of Georgia*'s toes) and chapter 6 with what are generally termed amusements, such as parks and movie theaters. What's the difference, you ask, for good reason? Six Flags Over Georgia could have fallen into either chapter, but the fact is that very few of the tourists who were passing through Georgia en route to Florida would have spent the time or money to stop at Six Flags in the same way they might for Rock City or Lion Country Safari. Therefore, Six Flags is considered an amusement and Frontier Lands is a tourist attraction. Don't worry if you can't keep them straight, as neither can I—and I'm the one who organized this whole silly thing.

ONE

FROM PEACHTREE STREET
TO MAIN STREET

A quick glance might lead one to believe this is New York's Times Square, but no, this is Atlanta's Peachtree Street during the 1960s. The giant signage for hometown hero Coca-Cola and broadcasting legend WSB Radio are the most prominent, but if you examine the background closely, you will find many others, including, at far right in the distance, the green rooftop sign of Rich's department store. In this chapter, we will visit many varied types of shopping, and Rich's seems like as good a place as any to begin.

Rich's was the unrivaled department store king in Atlanta, and eventually across several southern states. Its flagship store was legendary for its Christmas celebrations, including the "Great Tree" atop the glass-enclosed walkways that spanned Forsyth Street.

LEFT: After the 1924 Rich's flagship store closed in 1991, the huge building was converted into federal offices. Today, the only visible reminder of its glorious past is the original clock on the corner, which still bears its RICH'S ATLANTA letters replacing the twelve numerals of its less historic clock brethren. *Stephanie Stuckey collection.*

BELOW: A department store does not have to be a regional institution like Rich's to be important in retail history. The Ruben's store has been serving downtown Augusta since 1898, and its 1950s-style signage still exudes shopping bags full of appeal. *Stephanie Stuckey collection.*

ABOVE: Another fondly remembered type of shopping was the "variety store," formerly known as the "five and ten." These usually consisted of the founder's initials and last name, as pioneered by F.W. Woolworth. Here in downtown Atlanta, we see another example, J.J. Newberry, with its trademark aqua-colored façade. *From the American Geographical Society Library, University of Milwaukee–Wisconsin Libraries.*

OPPOSITE: Another "initials" variety store chain was H.L. Green. Its former location in Columbus has been transformed into a deli, but it is to the owners' credit that they chose to leave Green's signage (green, naturally) in place. *Stephanie Stuckey collection.*

During the 1960s, several of the old variety store companies began expanding into larger, more diversified "discount store" chains. S.S. Kresge morphed into Kmart, while F.W. Woolworth began its Woolco chain. And in the far left background of this 1972 Buford Highway view, you will see W.T. Grant's entry in the discount megastore race, Grant City. *Ron Sherman collection.*

TOP: Practically any photo of a downtown shopping district is going to include one of the Lerner Shop women's clothing stores, and that included Savannah. Here we also see the Manger Hotel (guests could write to their friends back home that they were away in the Manger) and a bespectacled mascot character perched on the digital clock for Home Federal Savings. *From the American Geographical Society Library, University of Milwaukee–Wisconsin Libraries.*

BOTTOM: Cartoon mascots for banks never became as popular as those for restaurants or cereal, but in addition to the Home Federal one we just saw, Decatur Federal Savings and Loan employed a mop-topped moppet known as Katy—no doubt an abbreviation for Decatur.

ABOVE: As the suburbs grew during the years immediately after World War II, the main shopping districts began shifting from the downtown city centers to new sprawling shopping centers and, later, shopping malls. This sign in Garden City, north of Savannah, is a reminder of when the one-stop shopping idea was a new one. *Debra Jane Seltzer collection.*

OPPOSITE: With more open space, the signs for suburban businesses could grow to sizes unheard of in downtown areas. This abandoned laundry enterprise was in the Atlanta suburb of Forest Park. *Debra Jane Seltzer collection.*

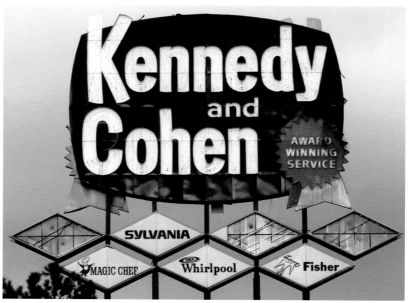

OPPOSITE, TOP: And speaking of laundry, how many of you remember the Norge laundromats with their polka-dotted globe emblems? Remnants of that once-common chain are scarce and even scarcer when they still carry their original lettering and color scheme. This one was still hanging around Dalton in 2007. *Debra Jane Seltzer collection.*

OPPOSITE, BOTTOM: Now here's an Atlanta business that sold every other major brand of appliance (even if Norge isn't listed on the surviving panels). Photographer Debra Jane Seltzer reports that this one-hundred-foot-tall monster had long outlived the store it advertised when she found it in 2006. *Debra Jane Seltzer collection.*

ABOVE: Drugstores were another necessary part of shopping, whether in large cities or small towns such as Abbeville, where this one was still proudly serving its purpose. And wherever there was a drugstore with a soda fountain, Coca-Cola was likely to be somewhere nearby. *Stephanie Stuckey collection.*

There were many fondly remembered brands of shoes for the seemingly endless market of children, and these neon masterpieces promoting one of those, Poll Parrot, were still there in 2006. No word on whether customers could pay for Poll Parrot Shoes with crackers instead of cash. *Debra Jane Seltzer collection.*

At least as of this writing, the Sewell Manufacturing Company was still in business, turning out men's clothing. Its former factory on U.S. 78 in Bremen now serves as a retail store, and these signs and the clock are believed to date back to the late 1920s.

Then, there are retail businesses that are not easily categorized. For example, enjoy this relic of another era that hung over a sidewalk in Macon. There were no doubt some deals to be found at Deal's, but the neon porter on the sign might have been the biggest deal of all. *John Margolies collection.*

Before photography became all digital, people needed places to buy film and have it developed. This crumbling relic near downtown Atlanta has certainly seen better days, but ironically, it continues to attract historians who preserve it, and its abandoned building below, with modern photographic technology never heard of while the shop was in business.

What reason could a real estate office have for using Uncle Remus and Brer Rabbit as its logo? How about the fact that it was based in Eatonton, the birthplace of author Joel Chandler Harris? Don't bother calling that phone number; this photo was taken in 1988, and the employees of Uncle Remus Realty have long since gone back to their briar patch.

OPPOSITE, TOP: "Mr. Builder" was the animated mascot for Giles Builders Supply in Albany. After Giles hung up its hammers and saws, Mr. Builder was sent to a retirement home at Albany's Thronateeska Heritage Foundation—the final resting place for some other signs we will encounter in pages hence. *Debra Jane Seltzer collection.*

OPPOSITE, BOTTOM: Antiques stores can be wonderful places to find vintage signs that were fortunate enough to be preserved after their useful life was over. Biggar Antiques in Chamblee was famous for its collection (not all of which originated in Georgia). Although no longer a retail store, Biggar still rents pieces of its collection for use as movie props. *Debra Jane Seltzer collection.*

ABOVE: The Braselton Bros. Department Store was obviously once the hub of activity in the town that shares its name. At the time of this 2013 photo, the former retailer had been converted into an antiques mall, but today the structure serves as a collection of boutique shops known as The 1904.

Okay, so this sign could apply to any antiques store in any town in any state. But it happened to be in Woodbine and attracted the attention of numerous photographers. Unfortunately, the Dead People's Things shop seems to now be deceased. *Russell Wells collection.*

TWO

HOME COOKING
MEETS FAST FOOD

In this chapter, we will be looking at the general topic of food, whether served in restaurants or cooked at home. This yummy nighttime shot from Skidaway Road in Savannah is a good place to start; it was the first in a chain of at least six Carey Hilliard's locations. Hungry yet? You will be—very soon. *Debra Jane Seltzer collection.*

Sometimes the subject of restaurants can be depressing, too. In 2010, this lonely signpost, with the name long since rusted away, stood over a moss-draped plot alongside U.S. 17 in Eulonia with no hint of how its former building might have looked. *Russell Wells collection.*

This monolith of roadside dining outlived its accompanying business long enough to become a landmark on U.S. 301 at Dover. Eventually, the property became a Dollar General (surprise, surprise), but reportedly the giant sign was preserved rather than becoming a Paradise lost. Any plans for its future use are still a mystery, however.

OPPOSITE, TOP: Now, here's a great example of the type of home cooking restaurant we were likely to encounter on any road trip in the days before the proliferation of chains. The Mimosa—likely named for the tree and not an alcoholic beverage—was on U.S. 1 at Baxley, and its postcard modestly proclaimed it "the home of good foods." We believe it. *Al Coleman collection.*

OPPOSITE, BOTTOM: With the popularity of westerns in movies and especially television, it was no wonder the Chuck Wagon Restaurant and Gift Shop on U.S. 301 in Sylvania embraced the theme like a cowboy sticks to his horse. It featured "a foot trail through the pines" and even pony rides. A few chapters from now, we'll see how the western theme asserted itself in some Georgia roadside attractions as well.

ABOVE: Your eyes aren't playing tricks—Minchew's Restaurant in Valdosta unashamedly copied the famous Holiday Inn "Great Sign," changing the proportions only enough to skirt the edges of trademark infringement. We'll be seeing examples of the real thing once we bed down in the motels chapter for the night.

ABOVE: Yeah, the sign maker in Macon might not have ever heard of "I before E except after C" when he crafted this neon beauty for Nu-Way "Weiners" in 1937. Despite the spelling error, it lived on to become what is believed to be the oldest surviving neon sign in town. *Debra Jane Seltzer collection.*

OPPOSITE, TOP: Imagine that you're tooling down U.S. 41 on the way to Florida and you spy, with your little eye, the clock on the Colonnade Restaurant sign in Cartersville, advising "Time to Eat." How could you possibly resist? But one does have to wonder about the postcard photographer who was so concerned with the rather nondescript building that they cut off the right-hand edge of the restaurant's name.

OPPOSITE, BOTTOM: There was no paucity of Georgia roadside businesses of all types that traded on the state's plantation heritage. Here we are at the Friendship Village Inn on U.S. 341 in Hazlehurst, which was primarily a motel but was also famous for its restaurant located in "the big house." That sort of imagery is rather frowned upon today.

OPPOSITE: At first glance, Augusta's chain of Wife Saver restaurants might also seem to be at odds with modern thinking, but the name has seemingly done no harm to their popularity. The logo of two lovebirds billing and cooing continues to represent the chicken/seafood combo eateries today. *Stephanie Stuckey collection.*

ABOVE: What represents southern cooking more than barbecue? The town of Gray sits on U.S. 129, yet another of the many north–south highways that cut through Georgia on the way to Florida. The Old Clinton Bar-B-Q was celebrating its fiftieth anniversary in 2008, and likely its beautiful pink and yellow neon had been around for about the same length of time. *Debra Jane Seltzer collection.*

LEFT: Well, yeah—any pig is going to turn red after being placed in a barbecue pit. This sign on U.S. 301 in Nahunta serves as our transition from sit-down restaurants to drive-ins, which enjoyed their own unique place in pop culture during the 1950s and 1960s. *John Margolies collection.*

BELOW: There's something disturbing about the enthusiasm shown by neon pigs for promoting cannibalism within the species. The Red Pig at the drive-in we just saw was calm enough serving one of his relatives on a plate, but at the Twin Oaks Drive-In in Brunswick, the pudgy porkers seemed to be dancing in positive ecstasy. *John Margolies collection.*

Quite a number of drive-ins in Georgia and many other states chose neon polar bears and ice cream cones instead of happy, doomed pigs. The Arctic Bear in Albany was one of that city's cultural touchstones, and as a result, the sign now resides at the aforementioned Thronateeska Heritage Foundation. You can't lick that! *Michael Sussman collection.*

OPPOSITE, TOP: The Georgia Girl Drive-In in Woodbine predates the hit song "Georgy Girl" (from the movie of the same name) by many years, but its sign has proved to have more sticking power than the tune. It was somewhat unusual for a sign to depict a southern belle chowing down on such a hearty meal. It has become a popular subject for roadside photographers, even as it has deteriorated further into illegibility. This shot is from 2010. *Russell Wells collection.*

OPPOSITE, BOTTOM: According to its official history, when Mary MacKenzie went into business in 1945, it was considered gauche for a woman to own a restaurant, so she named her establishment Mary Mac's Tea Room—even though it was still a restaurant. It continues its tradition of serving Atlanta to this day, whether hungry diners are looking for a restaurant or a tearoom. *Stephanie Stuckey collection.*

ABOVE: The sign at Sorry Charlie's Oyster Bar in Savannah is something of a Frankenstein monster. The colorful neon fish dates back to 1947, when it was the emblem for Mathews' Fish Market. Other parts of the sign were taken out and put back in as the business changed identities, and now it is possible that none of it is original. It's still an amazing sight, though. *Stephanie Stuckey collection.*

OPPOSITE: The S&S Cafeterias have been a Georgia tradition since 1936, with locations in many different cities. This particular one is in Augusta; in our final chapter, we will see an earlier version of S&S signage elsewhere. *Stephanie Stuckey collection.*

ABOVE: For many years, the king of all roadside restaurant chains was "host of the highways" Howard Johnson's. It was a leader in the concept of "building as sign," as its orange roofs and aqua spires were as identifiable from a distance as any sign could have been. But HoJo's did not neglect a traditional sign either, and this one on Atlanta's Buford Highway was still sporting its neon spectacular with Simple Simon and the Pieman in 1972. *Ron Sherman collection.*

ABOVE: One Georgia-grown national chain is Waffle House, which began in 1955 with a single store on U.S. 278 in Decatur. It has now been preserved as a museum of the company's history, with a faithful rendering of the original sign. Instead of today's familiar black letters on separate yellow squares, the 1955 version featured letters that appeared to be made of dripping syrup.

OPPOSITE: Historians have determined that a Davis House location in Atlanta was the first Kentucky Fried Chicken outlet to have one of the soon-to-be traditional striped pagoda roofs. We could not find a suitable photo of that store, but this KFC in East Point was still carrying the Davis House name as part of its signage in the early 1970s. Next door is the modernized Howard Johnson's sign, still orange and aqua but greatly simplified from the one we saw earlier. *From the American Geographical Society Library, University of Milwaukee–Wisconsin Libraries.*

TOP: So successful was Kentucky Fried Chicken's "building as sign" that even an abandoned former location is easy to identify. This one in Albany in 2007 still bore scars of its red and white stripes on the roof, although long since faded to rust and white instead. *Debra Jane Seltzer collection.*

BOTTOM: In the late 1970s, Kentucky Fried Chicken began phasing out the pagoda roof buildings, but for a while it still maintained the tradition in the form of a striped plastic pyramid on the front of the structure. Even that eventually went away, but this abandoned KFC in Eastman still had its mini pagoda in 2020.

Hoping to prove that Kentucky was not the only state that knew how to fry a bird, Maryland Fried Chicken was hatched in—no, not Maryland—Orlando, Florida. (We kid you not, chickies.) It eventually ended up with several locations in Georgia, most with variations of this same signage. *Stephanie Stuckey collection.*

If you run out of states for names of your fried chicken chain, how about using a part of the chicken instead? Wishbone Fried Chicken raised its giant ossified sign in numerous Georgia towns, including this one in Newnan. *Stephanie Stuckey collection.*

LEFT: Munching our way from fried chicken to roast beef, we come to Arby's and its famous "giant hat" sign composed of neon and chasing yellow incandescent bulbs. This style sign is not completely extinct but has become an endangered species due to the expense of maintaining the few that still exist. *Debra Jane Seltzer collection.*

BELOW: Even the interiors of the early Arby's buildings served as signs, with steers in the floors created by inlaid tile. There are probably even fewer of these than the tall hat signs, but a former Arby's in Decatur still has its artistic tile, which remained hidden under a later floor covering for many years. *Debra Jane Seltzer collection.*

As far as hamburgers are concerned, Chattanooga-based Krystal was one of the pioneers in that field. John Margolies found this Orange Bowl in Columbus circa 1980, with its white porcelain enamel and curved windows betraying its origin as an early Krystal; no doubt the colorful orange above the sign was formerly the company emblem, a shiny silver crystal ball. *John Margolies collection.*

By the time photographer Ron Sherman captured this view of Buford Highway in Atlanta in 1972, Burger King had largely phased out its original signage with the neon king sitting on a hamburger and holding a milkshake. That's the focal point from this angle, but peer into the distance and you'll see one of the original "dripping letters" Waffle House signs and, just beyond the jolly king, the revolving sign for an Enco service station just before that brand name became Exxon. *Ron Sherman collection.*

TOP: Hardee's cooked its delicious "charco-broiled" burgers in these distinctive buildings for only a short period of time, roughly 1965–70. They certainly fit the building-as-sign concept, and this one in Columbus had long since been converted to other uses. It now no longer exists. *Debra Jane Seltzer collection.*

BOTTOM: Wendy's has gone through a number of logos over the years and now no longer uses the "Old Fashioned Hamburgers" slogan. Nevertheless, this reminder of the chain's past, and the original rendition of pigtailed Wendy, was still on the job in Fort Oglethorpe in 2018.

Some logos just weren't thought out very well. The original Taco Bell sign probably puzzled most people as to what it was—a red and green worm, maybe? No, it was supposed to represent a serape-wrapped Mexican sleeping under his sombrero. This example in Savannah is believed to be the only remaining one in use. *Stephanie Stuckey collection.*

TOP: Krispy Kreme Doughnuts are a southern dessert, meal and fundraising tool all in one box. These original signs with the crowned double K's are becoming more and more scarce. At this Atlanta location, the building was destroyed by fire, but the sign stood firm, promising a return.

BOTTOM: This is how the Atlanta building would have looked if it hadn't burned. As the headquarters for the Augusta Film Office, it has been lovingly preserved, including the green roof and former neon crown on the pinnacle. *Stephanie Stuckey collection.*

Although not at a restaurant, this toothy peanut in Plains pays tribute to that town's most famous export, former president Jimmy Carter, and his infectious grin. Prez Peanut leads us into our next discussion concerning food products rather than the businesses that served them. *Stephanie Stuckey collection.*

As historians are quick to point out, Coca-Cola was not actually invented in Atlanta but moved its headquarters there early enough that the city is able to claim it. When the Underground Atlanta complex was opened in the early 1970s, this vintage sign was one of the attractions bringing the early twentieth century back to life.

TOP: The large economy-size Coca-Cola neon spectacular at Atlanta's Five Points intersection has been a landmark for what seems like forever; an earlier view of it led off our first chapter here. Still displaying the time and temperature, hopefully it will remain on duty far into the future. *Stephanie Stuckey collection.*

BOTTOM: Not all Coca-Cola signs were as flashy as the one in Atlanta. These boxy variations were quite common, and in the town of McRae, it served to commemorate the centennial of that community's bottling works. *Stephanie Stuckey collection.*

ABOVE: One of Coca-Cola's leading rivals was Royal Crown Cola, often abbreviated to simply RC. This sign hanging in Caldwell chose to employ both names for those who might have been familiar with only one or the other. *Stephanie Stuckey collection*.

OPPOSITE: Although this wax carton is not strictly a sign, no doubt there were indeed many signs displaying the southern belle mascot of the Miss Georgia Dairy in Atlanta.

This metal sign hanging on the side of a building in Kingsland is a bit unusual in featuring two brand names that most people would consider rivals in the bakery business: Holsum and Sunbeam. Be that as it may, it seems that Little Miss Sunbeam has not aged a day even as the rest of the world has moved into another century. *John Margolies collection.*

THREE
GEORGIA'S ON THE GO

In this chapter, we will be looking at signs and businesses associated with the automobile (and a few other forms of transportation as well). How better could we begin than with this 1960 view of the signs that greeted drivers on one of the early expressways heading into downtown Atlanta? And notice the road construction barrels that were already in place—and still blocking lanes of traffic today.

Now, all those cars on the road had to come from somewhere, and used car dealerships were the sources for many of them. Tillman Motors in Valdosta had a more or less typical sign for its type of operation, with the giant neon arrow pointing the way into the lot. *Debra Jane Seltzer collection.*

This unusual design is believed to have originally been constructed for a Savannah nightclub before going into the used car business. The oval ring would have been most appropriate for its longtime identity of Saturn Pre-Owned Autos; Rimtyme Custom Wheels is a more recent adaptation but probably not the last. *Stephanie Stuckey collection.*

TOP: What, you say we're out of gas already? Luckily for us, we have plenty of cheap choices for filling up. This well-preserved Gulf station could still be seen in Kingsland about twenty years after its building style had been discontinued. *John Margolies collection.*

BOTTOM: At Gulf, we were encouraged to "stop at the sign of the orange disk." At the Sinclair stations, we stopped at the sign of the green dinosaur. At the time of this photo in the eastern Atlanta suburbs, you could get Top Value Stamps along with your Dino brand gasoline. *Vintage Atlanta collection.*

"Discover America Best By Car"

GEORGIA
AND SOUTHEASTERN U.S.

PURE

UNION OIL COMPANY OF CALIFORNIA©

PURE *Firebird* **Gasoline**

So, you don't like orange or green? How about the clean blue and white of the Pure Oil signage, sometimes spiced up with a red neon arrow or the company's "Firebird" emblem? In the early 1970s, Pure outlets were converted over to Union 76 (so you got orange anyway), but over the last couple of decades, Pure has been making a comeback along the highways.

TOP: Pure and several other brands used a cottage-style building to make their gas stations stand out from the roadside clutter. American Oil (aka Amoco) was one of those, and if you squint hard, you will be able to make out the original American logo on this gable in Claxton, as seen in 2011. *Russell Wells collection.*

BOTTOM: You could trust your car to the man who wore the star—the big, bright Texaco star, remember? But it appears that at this former station, the cars have stopped permanently. According to photographer Russell Wells, it sat alongside Georgia Highway 46, which was once a main route from Macon to Savannah. *Russell Wells collection.*

Spur was a gasoline brand that seemed to be everywhere even without the help of catchy TV and radio commercials and jingles. This long-unused Spur pump was keeping a lonely vigil in Valdosta in the early 1980s. *John Margolies collection.*

TOP: In the days when all gas was cheap, there were brands that proudly promoted themselves as cheaper than the cheap. Along with Billups ("Fill Up with Billups") and Mutual (some people called it "rabbit gas" after its logo of a running hare), there was Saf-T-Oil, mostly forgotten except for this remaining neon sign in Cochran, where it must have once served travelers headed to or from Florida. *Stephanie Stuckey collection.*

BOTTOM: Some regional brands are all but forgotten. Dixie Gas, represented by the crossed Confederate flags on its signage, was a lost cause in Sautee by 2012. *Russell Wells collection.*

THIS PAGE: Taking its logo from a different conflict in U.S. history, Colonial Gas and its Minuteman silhouette were found by John Margolies in two different Georgia locales: the sign over the ruined pump on U.S. 17 in Waverly, and the rusty but readable billboard at St. Mary's, the last town before crossing the river of the same name into the Sunshine State. *Both, John Margolies collection.*

OPPOSITE: All those cars on the roads were accompanied by a seemingly endless convoy of truckers, helping move the nation's goods from Point A to Points B, C and on to Z. Truck stops became known as the places to get the best eats, and likely the Tower on U.S. 17 in Colesburg fell right in there. Naturally, Coca-Cola had to get into the act with a lollipop-shaped appendage to the main sign. *John Margolies collection.*

ABOVE: The Blue Bird Truck Stop was a very visible sight on I-20 in downtown Atlanta, even before there was such a name as I-20 (see *Lost Attractions of Georgia* for a look at the huge sign in its prime). After the Blue Bird signs flew the coop in 1994, one of the feathered friends was grounded behind the building, with rust eating at its pinfeathers. *Debra Jane Seltzer collection.*

LEFT: No car? No truck? How about taking the bus "and leaving the driving to us"? Columbus's Greyhound bus depot signage does seem to belong to another era somewhat, but that dog sure can run. *Stephanie Stuckey collection.*

BELOW: Finally, we come to air travel, which does not seem to bring out as many fond memories as those connected with road trips. However, the early 1960s view of the Atlanta airport terminal displays plenty of that aqua coloration that was so prevalent at the time, from public buildings to motels—which just happen to be the subject of our next chapter.

FOUR

WHEN IT'S SLEEPY TIME DOWN SOUTH

After all that driving, it's time to pick out a motel for the night. And possibly no other motel in Georgia embraces its deliberately outdated look more than the Thunderbird Inn in Savannah. It opened in 1964 and not only has resisted any urges to modernize but positively revels in its "retro" appearance. This eye-popping sign is only one element in its overall theme of lodging as it used to be. *Stephanie Stuckey collection.*

ABOVE: One might expect the Dutch Motel would have had as its roadside lure a windmill of the kind usually seen alongside rows of tulips in pictures of Holland. However, its windmill on U.S. 1 south of Augusta would have looked more at home on Uncle Henry's farm in Kansas.

OPPOSITE: Sometimes there is no good explanation for why a motel would be named after a famous storybook character. So it is with the Bambi Motel in Griffin, which appears to have been about ready for the taxidermist when this peeling sign was photographed, circa 1980. Perhaps man was in the forest, but Bambi no longer roams in Griffin. *John Margolies collection.*

BRER RABBIT MOTOR COURT
Dublin, Georgia

ABOVE: Brer Rabbit was one of Georgia's most renowned literary characters, but his primary laughing place was the area around Eatonton. Why Dublin, more than sixty miles south of Eatonton, chose to have a Brer Rabbit Motor Court remains a mystery. (In our next chapter, we will see more of Mr. Rabbit's influence in his hometown.)

OPPOSITE: Ordinarily, it would seem odd to find a Georgia motel named after storybook sweetheart Heidi, who hung out in the Swiss Alps. But when you consider that the town in question is Helen, which in 1969 adopted a new Bavarian/Alpine theme for the entire town, Heidi's "hidy-doo" is perfectly at home. *Russell Wells collection.*

OPPOSITE: People were staying in hotels long before the idea of roadside motels (a contraction for "motor hotels," for those who came in late). Atlanta's Hotel Clermont made its debut in 1939, although the building had existed as an apartment house even before that. The vertical neon letters on what was once a radio tower are an iconic part of its décor. *Debra Jane Seltzer collection.*

ABOVE: When Six Flags Over Georgia first opened in 1967, there were initially no motels within sight of its front gate. About the nearest was the Air Way Motel adjacent to the Fulton County Airport, approximately two and a half miles away. That was where this author and family stayed until the Six Flags neighborhood could develop its own crop of motels in the early 1970s. (I can still remember the "Air Way" part of the sign glowing with turquoise neon at night.)

THIS PAGE: Urban motels needed to attract a different type of client than the ones on major tourist highways. Atlanta's Downtown Motel relied on vertical signage and a rooftop display to be noticed in the crowded city streets; the Tech Motel's lettering was reminiscent of California coffeehouse graphic design.

It isn't hard to guess how this "altered" view came about. The Top Hat Motel tipped its topper to travelers along U.S. 41 in the Forest Park suburb of Atlanta. Apparently at some point there was an ownership/name change to the Plaza Motel, and rather than ditching a bunch of already-printed postcards, the new bosses simply rubber stamped the new name over the former one—rather clumsily, we might add.

Of course, all the motels in this chapter are Georgia motels, but Columbus made the point good and clear by having a true Georgian Motel—complete with the state map on its neon sign. It was showing its age when this photo was taken in 1982. *John Margolies collection.*

OPPOSITE, TOP: With its Valentine's Day motif, the Heart of Columbus Motel would have made an excellent spot for a honeymoon couple, hmm? It was on U.S. 280, which was alternately known as the Florida Short Route because it intersected with so many of the major north–south highways leading to that promised land. *Al Coleman collection.*

OPPOSITE, BOTTOM: Columbus's Candlelight Motel was already on the verge of being snuffed out at the time of this 2005 photo. As evidence, notice the semi-decayed curtains hanging in the lobby window; if it were actually still in business, those would be a good clue to tootle on down the road to the Heart of Columbus instead. *Debra Jane Seltzer collection.*

ABOVE: Today, it's hard to realize what a major tourist route U.S. 301 was before I-75 and I-95 were alternatives. We'll spend the next few pages among the many motels along 301, beginning with this one in Jesup. Just to show what a prime location that was supposed to be, the postcard indicates that Jesup is "just a day away" from Knoxville, Miami, Mobile, Pensacola, Roanoke, Rocky Mount, Raleigh, Palm Beach, Hollywood, Fort Myers, St. Petersburg and Tampa. Whew! *Al Coleman collection.*

THE
DON JUAN
MOTEL
Jesup,
Georgia

THE HACIENDA COURT . . . inside city limits on U. S. 301 and 25 . . . Jesup, Ga.

OPPOSITE: It's surprising that Jesup didn't advertise being only a day away from Mexico, considering these two Spanish-themed motels where travelers could take their siestas. Contrary to what you might think, the Don Juan and the Hacienda were not under common ownership, although both of their postcards were produced by the same company. (The Hacienda stated it was "on your direct route to Florida and the Golden Isles of Georgia.")

ABOVE: Now we're in Sylvania, another big motel market on 301. This postcard of the Syl-Va-Lane Motel and Restaurant was postmarked in Sylvania on February 17, 1964, and mailed to Pennsylvania. The writer noted that "the room we are in isn't on the picture." Oh well, that sign is the most interesting part of it anyway. *Al Coleman collection.*

OPPOSITE, TOP: The Holiday Motel and Restaurant complex was advertised as eleven miles south of Sylvania. Being out in the countryside probably explains the enormous front lawn, but that main office shaped like a southern plantation house was also a sight to see.

OPPOSITE, BOTTOM: Sylvania's Dreamland Motel was still slumbering along 301 in 2009, but current maps show it now rejoices under the more generic name of "Budget Motel." That usually isn't a good indicator of quality, but it's still a reminder of what travel on that highway once was. The restaurant next door is currently shown as a deer meat processing plant. *Russell Wells collection.*

ABOVE: The people who stayed at the Town House Motel on 301 in Glennville mailed this postcard home to New Hampshire on December 28, 1960. The reason for their trip is probably summed up in the one sentence: "Nice and warm; no coats." Too bad they didn't say whether that neon coach and horse on the sign were animated at night.

ABOVE: There were no palms in sight at the Palms Tourist Court in Claxton, but at least the name could remind visitors of the tropical wonderland that awaited them at the end of their journey. Of course, as the Scarecrow of Oz said, "People do go both ways," so those headed north might have a bittersweet memory of their vacation being almost over. *Al Coleman collection.*

OPPOSITE, TOP: Another primary north–south route was U.S. 41, bringing tourists from Chicago and Michigan. We've already seen one Georgian Motel in Columbus, but this sign for the Georgian Motor Court in Cordele was no doubt quite a few years older. As of 2023, the sign and former motor court were still there, more than forty years after it closed. *Debra Jane Seltzer collection.*

OPPOSITE, BOTTOM: Adel was one of the lucky U.S. 41 towns to have I-75 run alongside it, so it did not become as depressed as so many others that were completely bypassed. Although partly obscured by palm fronds, the bottom part of the sign claims, "Best Food on I-75 for Four Hours." Yes, that now-busy interstate was still somewhat underdeveloped even after the opening of Walt Disney World in late 1971. *Al Coleman collection.*

OPPOSITE: Now let's travel on U.S. 27 for a while. Those needing a place to spend the night in Blakely probably found the Quail Motel to be a bird in the hand. It's still there—but this particular sign isn't—for anyone who wishes to nest there for a while. *Debra Jane Seltzer collection.*

ABOVE: Valdosta is one of the last stops before U.S. 41 flows into Florida, and a number of people have no doubt gotten their jollies at the Jolly Inn, what with a rate of thirty-nine dollars per night and all. Its online reviews make it sound more gloomy than jolly, but they aren't geared toward people who would appreciate this huge signage, either. *Stephanie Stuckey collection.*

THIS PAGE: By the time U.S. 17 gets to Brunswick, it's almost to the Georgia coast. The Oak Park Inn was already gone by the time of this 2010 photo, leaving its sign guarding only some subtropical foliage. By contrast, the Oleander Motel is still in business but no longer has that huge A-frame structure to support its sign. *Both, Russell Wells collection.*

It's the return of corrugated yellow plastic: for a very brief period in the 1960s, the Stuckey's candy shops made a venture into the motel trade with a chain of Carriage Inns. They were scattered far and wide over multiple states, but this one on Jekyll Island was a personal favorite of the Stuckey family. *Stephanie Stuckey collection.*

OPPOSITE, TOP: The Stuckey's Carriage Inn sign was one of only eight chosen to represent Jekyll Island's numerous motels in this collage that appeared in a mid-1960s pamphlet. As you can see, Jekyll Island somewhat appeared to have all the other Georgia tourist routes combined into a single location.

OPPOSITE, BOTTOM: Moving from Georgia's beaches to the mountains, we arrive in Chatsworth and drop in at the Chief Vann Motel. Or at least its sign—the motel was long abandoned by the time of this photo. It appears that multiple repaint jobs might have altered Chief Vann's original appearance, but for sure the neon that once illuminated the sign was nowhere to be seen. *Debra Jane Seltzer collection.*

ABOVE: Here's a story of resurrection. The former Southland Motel on U.S. 11 in Trenton was empty for many years, a sad reminder of when that stretch of highway was a main approach into Chattanooga. The entrance arrow, which probably had a neon glow once, was the only signage left. But in 2021, the property was renovated and reopened as the Groovy Nomad Motel, with each room decorated in a different retro theme. Sometimes there is life in old roadside relics after all.

OPPOSITE: Up until now, we have mostly been talking about independent mom-and-pop motels. In the early 1950s, Holiday Inn pioneered the concept of a "no surprises" chain, and this rusting early depiction of the famous Holiday Inn "Great Sign" emerged from the overgrowth alongside U.S. 82 in 1992. The westbound side advertised 45 miles to Albany, while this eastbound side announced 150 miles to the Holiday Inn at Jacksonville (even though U.S. 82 ran nowhere near Florida).

ABOVE: This is how the Great Sign appeared after reaching its final and most familiar form. As you can see, it was situated at the city limits of East Point but was identical to thousands of other Great Signs all over the world. *From the American Geographical Society Library, University of Milwaukee–Wisconsin Libraries.*

McDONOUGH, GA.
I-75 and State 155
404-957-5291
LOCUST GROVE, GA.
I-75 and Locust Grove —
Hampton Exit
404-957-2601

McDONOUGH, GA.

LION COUNTRY SAFARI — JUST MINUTES AWAY

LOCUST GROVE, GA.

OPPOSITE: There was nothing out of the ordinary about the Holiday Inn near McDonough's short-lived Lion Country Safari attraction, but for some reason, its postcards chose to depict the Great Sign and the logo in a maroon color, rather than the official trademark of green.

THIS PAGE, TOP: This scene could have been anywhere, but it was the Holiday Inn in Waycross. By the 1960s, the sign and architectural features of most Holiday Inns had been standardized, including the restaurant that was usually as popular with locals as it was with travelers.

THIS PAGE, BOTTOM: The Charlton Motel in Folkston was unrelated to the magazine/comic book publisher of the same name. It was one of the many motels that got cozy with a Howard Johnson's restaurant next door, a concept that would lead to the birth of a new lodging chain in Georgia. *Al Coleman collection.*

After years of constructing restaurants adjoining other owners' motels, in 1954, Howard Johnson's took its cue from Holiday Inn and opened the company's first Motor Lodge in Savannah. As you can see from this early postcard view, there was little to distinguish the lodge from all the other motels. That was about to change.

Since it would have been impractical to extend the trademark orange roofs to the Howard Johnson's Motor Lodges, the company did the next best thing and began constructing the main office of each motel in this more-than-distinctive style. This particular example was in Cordele, but the architecture of the "Gate Lodges," as they were dubbed, always makes them easy to identify today, even if abandoned or converted into other usage.

ABOVE AND OPPOSITE: The chain of Alamo Plaza Hotel Courts, in the ongoing race for roadside distinction, fronted its buildings with façades resembling the eponymous Texas landmark. The Alamo Plaza in Savannah, built in 1955, was a most elaborate example of the theme. Although a bit worse for wear, it still looks like a bit of San Antonio transplanted to Georgia today. *Both, John Margolies collection.*

ABOVE: Earlier, we mentioned the lack of motels in the immediate vicinity of Six Flags when that theme park opened in 1967. One chain that soon remedied that oversight was Mark Inns, which built not only a facility at one of the Six Flags exits but also nine more situated across the Atlanta metro area. And who could resist that lady giving potential lodgers a come-hither glance?

OPPOSITE: Remember the elegant Ramada Inn sign, with portly butler Uncle Ben announcing the name of the motel on his extra-long trumpet? Along with Holiday Inn's colonial innkeeper John Holiday and TraveLodge's sleepwalking Sleepy Bear, he was one of the most identifiable mascot characters in the hospitality industry.

THIS PAGE: For those outdoorsy types who preferred not to be cooped up in an air-conditioned motel room, there were campgrounds such as the Cherokee on Jekyll Island and the chain of KOA Kampgrounds (this one at Lake Park). Both used Native American imagery in their signage, but KOA also had its emblematic A-frame office building that vaguely reflected the tepee-shaped logo on the sign. Many such campgrounds did their best to have all the necessary amenities on the property, as listed on the Cherokee sign.

FIVE

THE GREAT GEORGIA ROADSIDE

Now we'll sample some of Georgia's classic roadside attraction signage, and what better sign to begin with than this geometric wonder on U.S. 1? But wait—take a close look at the Florida's Silver Springs sign in the inset photo. Although there is no firm evidence after so many years, it certainly appears that after Silver Springs ditched that sign for a more elaborate one in the early 1960s, the original made a journey from Ocala to Waycross and set up shop at the "land of trembling earth."

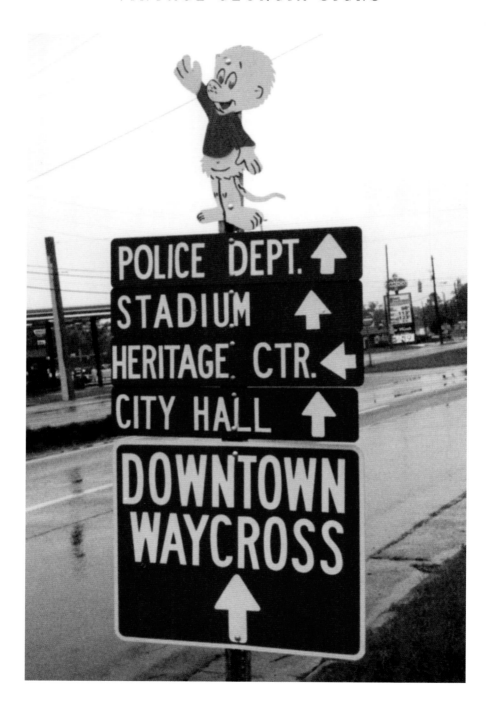

OPPOSITE: Waycross being home to the Okefenokee Swamp, and that marsh's most famous fictional resident being comic strip character Pogo Possum, in the 1990s, the city made a deal with cartoonist Walt Kelly's widow Selby to use Pogo in promoting the town. Here he is waving from one of the municipal direction signs in 1992.

ABOVE: From the swamps of southern Georgia, we jump to the mountains of the northwestern corner and find ourselves at the national park commemorating the Battle of Chickamauga during the Civil War. Most of the monuments relating to that part of the conflict are across the state line in Tennessee, but Chickamauga was established in 1898, just over thirty years after the battle.

TOP: There were Wild West–themed attractions all over the nation, especially during the craze for TV westerns in the late 1950s and early 1960s. Coming along a bit after the bloom was off the sagebrush was this one at Warm Springs known as Old Bullochville. It was a project of Paul Bolstein, an entrepreneur who had previously assisted with other such parks in Florida. Old Bullochville lasted about as long as the outlaw facing Marshal Dillon in the *Gunsmoke* opening titles.

BOTTOM: Cowboys and outlaws also roamed the streets of Frontier Lands on Fort Mountain near Chatsworth—but not for very long. Fort Mountain is now a Georgia state park, and the western characters moved on down the trail to wherever old cowpokes go. The logo on this souvenir pennant also appeared on the park's signage for as long as it lasted.

The view from Tallulah Point has been getting travelers on U.S. 23 to pull over for a look-see for years. In this vintage view, we can see not only the attraction's own signage but also the classic Coca-Cola "button" signs at the restaurant conveniently located next door. Smelling tourists and their money, there was also a Stuckey's nearby.

The Old Sautee Country Store is still holding its own after approximately 150 years, although it now has different vintage signs than the ones visible in this postcard. As an aside, the community in which it is located, now designated as Sautee Nacoochee, is named after the two (likely fictional) protagonists of the legend of Rock City's Lover's Leap, some 135 miles to the west—but that's literally another story.

ABOVE: Several pages ago, we saw a collection of signs representing the many beach motels available on Jekyll Island. This is the sight that greeted visitors as they entered that former playground for the rich—or, as one alleged wit put it, Jekyll Island is where the millionaires went to hyde. Heavens to Rockefeller!

OPPOSITE: With the roadside attraction industry seemingly obsessed with the "world's largest" something or other, why not have the World's Largest World? Savannah is the home of the globular giant, which is actually a natural gas storage tank. When first painted in 1956, it looked like this brochure, with latitude and longitude lines. Later repaintings eliminated the cartographic elements and added a hurricane approaching the Georgia coast from the east.

See
The World's Largest World

LOCATED ON BULL STREET AT DeRENNE AVENUE

An Easy 10 Minute Drive
from Downtown Historic Savannah

OPPOSITE: Earlier we mentioned the 1969 development of the Underground Atlanta complex. This view from its early days shows a number of the nostalgic signs that were included; some might have been re-creations of originals, but most were simply attempting to capture the flavor of the bygone gaslight era.

ABOVE: One of the many attractions in Underground Atlanta was the Tussaud Wax Museum. Now, many wax museums can seem more than a little creepy, but have you ever seen anything to compare with the cadaverous Rhett and Scarlett staring blankly out the front window with their sightless eyes? This was the type of attraction likely to induce nightmares, even in the daytime.

And speaking of characters with creepy faces, we come to the Cabbage Patch Kids Babyland General Hospital in Cleveland. Although it seems like a more recent addition to the roadside scene, it actually dates back to 1978. Craftsman Xavier Roberts's melon-headed creations did not hit the big time until the 1983 Christmas season, when they produced plenty of violence in stores instead of peace on earth. Their popularity has waxed and waned ever since, but Babyland General is still there, hoping another craze will break out. *Stephanie Stuckey collection.*

THIS PAGE: From the cabbage patch we hop on over to the briar patch, where that famous folk tale trickster Brer Rabbit hangs out in Eatonton, the hometown of author Joel Chandler Harris. The statue of Brother Rodent cannot be truly considered a sign but has been the emblem of the town on the county courthouse lawn for longer than anyone can remember. A replica stands in front of the Uncle Remus Museum, which was displaying this attention-grabbing entrance sign in 1989.

ABOVE: Although Harris was born in Eatonton, most of his career as a writer was spent at this home he moved into in Atlanta's far western city limits in 1881. He named it the Wren's Nest after a feathered family was found to have established a home in the mailbox. This arched sign was in place by the early 1970s. The house remains a cultural center, with many programs educating local schoolkids about the folk tale tradition.

OPPOSITE: Since Stone Mountain Park was operated by the state for most of its career, its on-site signage was usually low-key. In the early days, the emphasis was on the Stone Mountain Scenic Railroad, an element that could have been found in most theme parks. The round, rusting metal railroad sign was discovered in the trash by a former park employee; its eventual fate is unknown.

What could be the significance of this hand-lettered triangular sign? In the 1960s and 1970s, when the re-created antebellum plantation at Stone Mountain Park was known as Stone Acres, it boasted periodic visits from Hollywood star Butterfly McQueen, best known as the hysterical "Prissy" of *Gone with the Wind*. This sign would be hung outside on the days she was present to receive guests. Like the metal railroad sign, its current whereabouts are a mystery.

Lion Country Safari, part of a chain of drive-through attractions with other locations in California, Ohio and Florida, opened its jaws to visitors in McDonough in 1972. The entrance would have been difficult to ignore with tusks this size towering over any cars turning into the driveway.

Everything at Lion Country Safari was at least intended to give the impression of an outpost in Africa. In the background of this shot, notice the sign advertising film, something that might have been hard to come by in the real jungle or African veldt. *David M. Smith collection.*

126

OPPOSITE: The aforementioned Rock City Gardens, which may or may not have once been home to Sautee and Nacoochee, is usually thought of as a Chattanooga attraction, but geographically it sits across the state line in Georgia. That's yours truly on his first visit there in 1967; the colorful framed sign was installed in the entrance court for camera-toting tourists to use as a title frame for their slides or home movies.

ABOVE: To its credit, Rock City remains one of the most unchanged tourist attractions in any state. These two photos illustrate one of the man-made elements that was allowed to go away over the decades: the twisted metal signs spelling out the gardens' sights in cursive lettering. In the moonshine still scene, the identifying sign was painted with fluorescent colors so it appeared to glow like neon under a black light tube in the rear of the cavern.

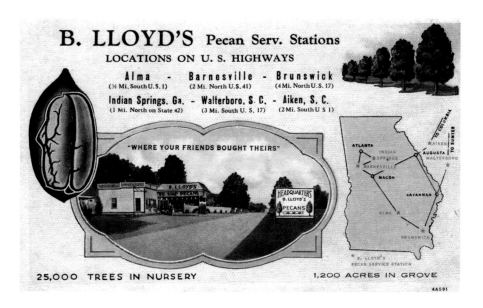

ABOVE: Now we turn our attention to some of the businesses that existed mainly to sell candy and souvenirs to tourists. By the time of this 1934 postcard, the chain of B. Lloyd's Pecan Service Stations had expanded to four locations in Georgia and a couple of outliers in South Carolina. B. Lloyd's would soon be eclipsed by an even larger chain that came to represent the southern roadside from coast to coast.

OPPOSITE, TOP: When W.S. Stuckey began selling pecans—and subsequently, pecan candy—from a roadside stand in Eastman around 1935, he could not have known what an institution his business would become. In 1952, this massive complex was built as Stuckey's candy factory and corporate office—and as you can see, it was the first thing drivers entering the city limits of Eastman would see. *Stephanie Stuckey collection.*

OPPOSITE, BOTTOM: Throughout the 1950s, this was the standard design for the Stuckey's stores. This particular building was on U.S. 301 at Statesboro, but nearly all of them had the same pink color scheme and mural promising cold orange juice, a necessity for those heading to or from Florida in non-air-conditioned cars.

ABOVE: Time for more corrugated yellow plastic: this unusually huge example of the Stuckey's logo was being hoisted into place in a location that was, unfortunately, not documented by the photographer's records. Its atypical size and shape hint that it might have been destined for one of the short-lived Carriage Inn locations. *Stephanie Stuckey collection.*

OPPOSITE, TOP: In the early 1960s, the Stuckey's buildings evolved into this sloped-roof style, the tiles painted a bright turquoise color. This was the building that replaced the original 1930s store in Eastman, adjacent to the corporate office. As traffic was siphoned away by interstate highways, it suffered the indignity of becoming a succession of non-pecan-candy businesses; at the time of this photo, it was serving as a steakhouse. *Russell Wells collection.*

OPPOSITE, BOTTOM: Occasionally, former Stuckey's buildings simply assumed new names and continued to operate with the same mix of candy and souvenirs as they had before. If not for the change in signage, Sands Pecans on U.S. 301 in Glennville could have passed for a less colorful unit in the Stuckey's chain.

THIS PAGE: Some Georgia pecan stands could not resist the urge to "borrow" Stuckey's famous yellow and red signage. John Margolies found the almost-obscured billboard for Rawl's Pecans on U.S. 17 (the location of the store itself was no longer visible). Randy's, on U.S. 1 at Folkston, was another example that aped not only the color scheme but Stuckey's logo lettering as well. *Top, John Margolies collection.*

In the 1960s and early 1970s, Stuckey's biggest competitor was one that did not copy its logo in the least. Horne's stores were all up and down the major routes to Florida, replacing Stuckey's turquoise roofs with shiny yellow tiles. You are going to have to look very carefully, but if you peer hard, you should be able to make out the faded Horne's lettering on the front of this portico. Ironically, the yellow roof was still glinting in the sun. *Russell Wells collection.*

Looking like Stuckey's or Horne's on steroids, the enormous Magnolia Plantation pecan candy/souvenirs/gas station has been a landmark on I-75 at Tifton for decades. About an hour north of the Florida state line, it's a logical stop for those who are about to go nuts from the boring interstate drive. And no, we don't know the identity of the Georgia peach posing in this early Magnolia Plantation postcard.

When it comes to candy shops, why not ask an expert? The Hansel and Gretel Candy Kitchen in Helen has been cooking up goodies—but hopefully not wicked witches—in its ovens since 1973. The setting of its namesake bedtime story might not strictly fit the town's Alpine theme, but the architecture and painted mural on the wall certainly do. *Russell Wells collection.*

21 MOTHER GOOSE EXHIBITS
LIFE SIZE • TALKING • EXCITING
6 AMUSEMENT RIDES
ADMISSION 50c • FREE PARKING
Fun for all ages! See page 28.
FREE PICNIC FACILITIES

Enter **Storyland**

● On H'way 41 — 6 mi. South of Marietta & 1 mi. North of Atlanta City Limits ●

World Famous **BATTLE-RAMA** *Open Daily!* (AAA)

DIRECTLY ON U.S. 41 — 20 MILES NORTH OF ATLANTA

World's Largest Civil War Diorama ● Over 20,000 Handmade Pieces ● See The Battle of Atlanta ● See The Battle of Kennesaw Mtn. ● Hear Dr. Bell I. Wiley, Famous Author ● PLUS Georgia's Finest Civil War Museum ● Souvenirs, Relics, Old Guns, Refreshments ● Adm. 75c, Children 50c, Under 6 Free

EDUCATIONAL ● **A CIVIL WAR CENTENNIAL MUST** ● SEE PAGE 28

GEORGIA GAME PARK
—ON U.S. HIGHWAY 11, 25 MI. SOUTH OF CHATTANOOGA AT RISING FAWN, GA.—

FREAK ANIMALS
WILD ANIMALS
LIONS, BEARS, ETC.

SHELL PRODUCTS
FREE SOUVENIR WITH
EACH GAS FILL UP

2 LARGE SOUVENIR SHOPS
CHENILLE BEDSPREADS
CIDER BAR
FRIED MARBLES
FILM (3 ROLLS $1.00)

Finally, here are three miscellaneous attractions that were advertised all on the same page in a May 1963 visitors' guide. Storyland in Marietta is today almost as much a fairy tale as the scenes it depicted, so scarce is any documentation of its existence. The Battle-Rama at Kennesaw was yet another of those miniature battlefields with tiny soldiers acting out their historical conflict. And the Georgia Game Park was still at its original U.S. 11 location at Rising Fawn in 1963; once I-59 moved traffic a few miles to the west, the game park moved its zoo and freak animal displays ("See the two-headed snake!") to the new highway.

SIX

THE LANDS OF PLAY

We'll wrap up this long retrospective by visiting some of the places people went for amusement. Earlier photos show the Playland Skating Center sitting in relative isolation alongside Atlanta's Buford Highway, but by the time of this 1972 view, it was rapidly being hemmed in by gas stations and a golf driving range. The neon Sonja Henie lookalike on the sign would seem to fit ice skating more than roller skates. *Ron Sherman collection.*

ABOVE: Atlanta's Funtown Amusement Center is today largely known for its mention in a Martin Luther King speech, correctly identifying it as one of the places his daughters could not visit in the South's segregation days. After that period was over, Funtown survived for several more years, but its parts closed down one by one until only picturesque ruins were left. *Vintage Atlanta collection.*

OPPOSITE: One thing that caused the death of earlier, small amusement parks such as Funtown was the arrival of the huge Six Flags Over Georgia theme park in 1967. Oddly, in its earliest days, Six Flags did not have an official entrance sign. In 1969, it inherited the giant Sky Hook ride from its sister park in Texas, and the enormous Six Flags logo finally had a place to announce the park's presence to the world. *Andy Duckett collection.*

OPPOSITE, TOP: One of Six Flags' opening day attractions was the Hanson Car ride in the British section of the park. The antique cars and their original entrance building were still in place in 1985, although on the right-hand side you may be able to see the Highland Swing ride beginning to encroach on their bailiwick. The Hanson cars eventually relocated to the carousel/Cotton States Exposition region of Six Flags.

OPPOSITE, BOTTOM: Another pioneering Six Flags attraction, in more ways than one, was Jean Ribaut's Adventure. Basically the equivalent to Disneyland's Jungle Cruise, the Ribaut riverboat ride took visitors on a narrated journey through events in early Georgia history. This building with the sign served as the queue house; when the Ribaut ride became a part of history itself, the structure was converted into an observation deck for the Thunder River whitewater ride.

ABOVE: Six Flags' performing porpoise show, starring Skipper and Dolly, was a big hit from opening day. Its billboard-style signage changed over the years but always gave top billing to those two miraculous mammals. *Tim Campbell collection.*

OPPOSITE, TOP: In the exact center of the park was Tales of the Okefenokee, a dark ride through the "old plantation legends" we have previously seen in Eatonton and at the Wren's Nest. During that initial 1967 season, the exterior of the building was decorated with these painted signs illustrating the folk tale characters to be seen therein.

OPPOSITE, BOTTOM: Before the 1968 season, the Okefenokee scenes were totally revamped by famed puppeteers Sid and Marty Krofft, who enjoyed a cozy and symbiotic relationship with Six Flags. Their new character designs, considerably more cartoonish than the originals, were re-created in this new series of painted signs on the front lawn.

ABOVE: After the 1980 season, the interior of the Okefenokee building was gutted, and new scenes replaced the folk tale animals. Now it was the Monster Plantation, and in case anyone wondered what this strange new world was all about, this incredible sign at the entrance provided the backstory in great detail.

OPPOSITE: During one renovation of the Monster Plantation, this sign masquerading as a painting was placed in a somewhat hidden location in one of the first scenes. It subtly paid tribute to the ride's original persona by using renderings based on the 1968 Krofft character designs.

ABOVE: Speaking of the brothers Krofft, from opening day, they staged elaborate puppet shows in this theater in the USA, or "modern" section of the park. This façade depicting different forms of puppetry from around the world was installed in 1968 and remained unchanged until the Kroffts left to pursue other projects after the 1974 season.

The former Krofft Puppet Theater went through a succession of identities and signage over the years that followed; by 1985, it was serving as the home for a stage show featuring the immortal Looney Tunes cartoon characters. Compare this with the previous photo to see how many of the building's structural elements survived its changing usage.

Also in Six Flags' USA section was the Happy Motoring Freeway, the miniature auto ride sponsored by the Humble Oil Company as it evolved through brand names Esso, Enco and finally Exxon. Perched above the right-hand end, notice one of the fiberglass tigers ("Put a tiger in your tank!") that could also be seen at certain fortunate Humble Oil gas stations of the 1960s and early 1970s. *Nelson Boyd collection.*

Now for another category of signs that promised worlds of entertainment: theaters. For some fifty years, two of downtown Atlanta's prized movie palaces were the Paramount and Loew's Grand, seen here in 1950. The Paramount bit the carpet first, ten years after this photo. Loew's Grand ensured its place in movie history when it hosted the world premiere of *Gone with the Wind* in 1939, but those days were long over by 1978, when it closed after a disastrous fire and was subsequently demolished. *Vintage Atlanta collection.*

OPPOSITE: Atlanta's Fox Theater came perilously close to suffering the same fate as the Paramount and Loew's. It, too, hosted a lavish movie premiere, that for Walt Disney's *Song of the South* in 1946. After closing in 1974, the grand old 1929 palace was facing the wrecking ball. An appeal to the public saved the day, and the Fox is still one of the jewels in downtown Atlanta's crown.

ABOVE: The Plaza Theatre is about a decade younger than the Fox, opening in an early shopping center on U.S. 78 just east of downtown Atlanta in 1939. As indicated by this photo, the Plaza still serves its original function, showing the latest hit blockbusters. Its neon sign, and several others in the pre–World War II strip center, still glows brightly.

TOP: This aerial view of Savannah could have gone into other chapters, but it is included here for its unusual view of the Savannah Theater's marquee on the back corner of the building, rather than the front. Nearby, notice the billboards for 7Up and a brand of tires and one-third of a Texaco service station sign on a green-roofed building. In the distance is the Manger Hotel we visited many pages ago.

BOTTOM: The summer of 1975 was a study in contrasts in Augusta. One theater (the Imperial) was showing a movie that was the season's biggest smash, *Jaws*; a few doors down, the Modjeska was showing a double feature that wasn't, *Six Pack Annie* and *The Dirtiest Girl I Ever Met*. (Fun for the family, huh?) Somehow, one of the S&S Cafeterias was managing to hang on in the neighborhood, serving fans of great white sharks and dirty girls alike. *From the American Geographical Society Library, University of Milwaukee–Wisconsin Libraries.*

Practically every town, large or small, had its own theater during Hollywood's golden age. In Newnan, citizens remember the Alamo—or actually, have never forgotten it, since it still serves as a combination music venue and restaurant. *Stephanie Stuckey collection.*

OPPOSITE, TOP: The small town of Harlem rightfully prides itself on being the hometown of portly Oliver Hardy, longtime partner of Stan Laurel. The Columbia Theater did not exist during the years Hardy lived there; not opened until 1949, it even missed the entire span of time Laurel and Hardy were making their classic comedy films. Nevertheless, notice the mural commemorating the hilarious team on the exterior wall. *Russell Wells collection.*

OPPOSITE, BOTTOM: Our featured towns and theaters keep getting smaller. This abandoned shell could still be seen in Kingsland around 1980 but appeared to be in no condition to show movies. Being in Georgia, it should be no surprise that a Coca-Cola advertisement stubbornly clung to the front even as the rest of the building was crumbling around it. The former theater later served as an apartment building. *John Margolies collection.*

ABOVE: Then, there was the drive-in variety of theater, which generally expired even sooner than its indoor cousins. The Cairo Drive-In Theater—in the town of the same name, of course, not Egypt—still had its sign on the back of the giant screen in 1979, but not for much longer. *John Margolies collection.*

Many images in this book could have served as our farewell, but the North 53 Drive-In at Rome—on the highway of the same name—seems to be as good a choice as any. Instead of a movie title, the CLOSED letters on the marquee seem evocative of an era. And since the North 53 is closed, we can now close our tour as well. *John Margolies collection.*

BIBLIOGRAPHY

Clemmons, Jeff. *Rich's: A Southern Tradition*. Charleston, SC: The History Press, 2012.

Hollis, Tim. *Images of America: Six Flags Over Georgia*. Charleston, SC: Arcadia Publishing, 2006.

———. *Lost Attractions of Georgia*. Charleston, SC: The History Press, 2021.

———. *Stuckey's*. Charleston, SC: Arcadia Publishing, 2017.

Jakle, John A., and Keith A. Sculle. *Fast Food: Roadside Restaurants in the Automobile Age*. Baltimore, MD: Johns Hopkins University Press, 1999.

———. *The Gas Station in America*. Baltimore, MD: Johns Hopkins University Press, 1994.

Jakle, John A., Keith A. Sculle and Jefferson S. Rogers. *The Motel in America*. Baltimore, MD: Johns Hopkins University Press, 1996.

Kirby, Doug, Ken Smith and Mike Wilkins. *The New Roadside America*. New York: Simon and Schuster, 1992.

Langdon, Philip. *Orange Roofs, Golden Arches: The Architecture of America's Chain Restaurants*. New York: Alfred A. Knopf, 1986.

Margolies, John, and Emily Gwathney. *Signs of Our Time*. New York: Abbeville Press, 1993.

ABOUT THE AUTHOR

Tim Hollis has written thirty-nine other books on pop culture history, a number of them concerning southeastern tourism. He also operates his own museum of vintage toys, souvenirs and other pop culture artifacts near Birmingham, Alabama.